YOUR KNOWLEDGE HAS

- We will publish your bachelor's and master's thesis, essays and papers

- Your own eBook and book - sold worldwide in all relevant shops

- Earn money with each sale

Upload your text at www.GRIN.com
and publish for free

Nicholas Guantai

Cloud Computing Business in Saudi Arabia

An Examination of the Feasibility of Public Cloud Computing by Enterprise Businesses

GRIN Verlag

Bibliografische Information der Deutschen Nationalbibliothek:

Die Deutsche Bibliothek verzeichnet diese Publikation in der Deutschen National-
bibliografie; detaillierte bibliografische Daten sind im Internet über http://dnb.d-
nb.de/ abrufbar.

Imprint:

Copyright © 2014 GRIN Verlag GmbH
Druck und Bindung: Books on Demand GmbH, Norderstedt Germany
ISBN: 978-3-656-70014-2

GRIN - Your knowledge has value

Der GRIN Verlag publiziert seit 1998 wissenschaftliche Arbeiten von Studenten, Hochschullehrern und anderen Akademikern als eBook und gedrucktes Buch. Die Verlagswebsite www.grin.com ist die ideale Plattform zur Veröffentlichung von Hausarbeiten, Abschlussarbeiten, wissenschaftlichen Aufsätzen, Dissertationen und Fachbüchern.

Visit us on the internet:

http://www.grin.com/

http://www.facebook.com/grincom

http://www.twitter.com/grin_com

Table of Contents

1

EXECUTIVE SUMMARY

Cloud computing has 3 primary service models including SaaS, IaaS and PaaS, which are classified depending on the level for which a service user interacts with the service provider's systems in accessing memory, processing power and storage. Deployment models of cloud computing include hybrid, community, public and private clouds depending on the approach to hosting and the number of clients sharing a resource. Due to the prohibitive nature of private cloud computing and requirement for specialized systems in community clouds, the most suitable approach to cloud computing for small and medium enterprises is public cloud computing. In this regard, this study was aimed at determining the extent to which implementation of public cloud computing by enterprise companies is feasible. Due to the cultural and the absence of law in Saudi Arabia ensuring the protection of data in the cloud, challenges in implementing cloud computing in the country are related to adherence to the data governance structure. For instance, privacy and security are important for enterprise companies since the local culture values the safeguarding of family and individual information. In addition, information transferred through the cloud system must adhere to the conservative philosophy and data privacy, which limits the level of compatibility in cloud computing between Saudi Arabia and the western world. Since most service providers are based in the west, companies have to identify a service provider that tailors its products to suit the market in Saudi Arabia. Therefore, implementation of public cloud computing in Saudi Arabia is feasible as long as companies select a service provider with a positive reputation, limit posting of sensitive information to the cloud server, and implement cloud computing gradually to avert the possibility of complete failure. This study determined that SaaS cloud computing is feasible for enterprise companies in Saudi Arabia, but further study is required to examine the feasibility of IaaS and PaaS. In addition, a larger study should be done to collect quantitative data to determine the implications of cloud computing in a representative sample.

Key to Abbreviations

SaaS: Software as a Service

IaaS: Infrastructure as a Service

PaaS: Platform as a Service

HaaS: Hardware as a Service

DaaS: Desktop as a Service

CaaS: Communications as a Service

OS: Operating System

PDA: Personal Digital Assistant

IT: Information Technology

NIST: National Institute of Standards and Technology (United Stated of America)

EC2: Amazon Elastic Compute Cloud service

DISA: Defense Information Systems Agency (United Stated of America)

CRM: Customer Relationship Management

SLA: Service Level Agreement

HIPAA: Health Insurance Portability and Accountability Act of 1996 - Privacy, Security and Breach Notification Rules

PCI DSS: Payment Card Industry Data Security Standard

CHAPTER 1: INTRODUCTION

Use of technology in business processes and functions has been evolving rapidly and consistently over time, and, in order to businesses to remain locally and globally competitive, they need to adjust their internal structures to keep up with these changes. In the early stages of information technology adoption by businesses, computers played a minor role in handling tasks that could easily be completed by employees. However, the information technology industry has undergone developments that have advanced the usage of computing devices beyond the limitations of a single workstation position (Hugos & Hulitzky, 2010). The capabilities and abilities of a workstation can be expanded for it to work as part of a much larger system with more computing power. In a cloud computing setup, a mainframe computer does most of the computing and storage tasks while workstations work as terminals accessing it through an intranet or the Internet depending on the type of cloud in use. In this regard, cloud computing is an advanced combination of technologies developed over time with the intention of increasing computing security, availability, affordability, portability, and connectivity (Buyya, et al., 2011). These technologies include encryption technologies, networking technologies and various other technologies whose combined effects is to reduce the costs while addressing the computing needs of the person or organization.

While cloud computing has multiple applications at a consumer level as a computational and backup tool, applications in business enterprise are virtually unlimited due to the versatility of the approach in information technology implementation. Several market leaders including Google, Microsoft, IBM, Lenovo and Apple have invested heavily as cloud computing service providers with the aim of increasing their earnings from this emerging technology that shows great potential (Grant AE & Meadows JH, p. 181). Computer vendors have designed consumer products with limited functionality, whose primary purpose is to act as terminals for primarily cloud-based computing. For instance, Google, in collaboration with computer vendors worldwide, has come up with ChromeBooks, which are computers with limited storage and processing power that are built to work with Chrome OS. According to (Karabek, 2011), the potential benefits of cloud computing have resulted in widespread adoption of cloud computing, and research is necessary to determine the best approach to cloud computing for business entities.

1.1 Statement of the Problem

Cloud computing can be implemented through multiple models including private cloud, public cloud and hybrid cloud, and their derivatives like community cloud and distributed cloud depending on service provider, users and deployment approach (Hausman, 2013). Due to the obvious benefits of cloud computing, enterprise companies have to implement cloud computing to make data collection, storage,

5

processing, manipulation and communication an integrative process (Stair, 2010). However, with so many options to deployment options, and varying advantages and shortcomings of cloud computing models, companies have to perform a clear assessment of their needs in order to choose the most appropriate of the many cloud computing models. Different business entities have varying knowledge and information management approaches, which necessitates the application of a cloud computing approach that is most appropriate for their needs. On one hand, some companies may need specialized technologies in order to perform specialized tasks that are not available in public cloud computing, which necessitates the adoption of a private cloud computing approach. On the other hand, some companies may not have the resources to invest in the purchase of servers and other technologies required to implement a private cloud computing approach, and such a company would benefit from the storage and computing power offered by public clouds. Moreover, some companies may have resources to invest in a private cloud but also need the benefits of the public cloud, and such companies tend to favor a hybrid cloud computing system. Therefore, the choice of cloud computing deployment approach by a business entity depends on the cost and functional benefits of the approach, and the computing needs of the business entity.

1.2 Purpose and Significance of the Study

Investing in cloud computing poses a challenge for enterprise companies, especially since companies have to choose the best approach to cloud computing deployment that will address their needs and expectations with maximum benefits and minimal costs (Karabek, 2011). In this regard, companies must first determine their needs in terms of data management, and identify the most suitable cloud computing approach from the available private, public cloud, hybrid, community, and distributed cloud choices. For instance, although large cloud providers have the resources and technology to provide high quality services, access to these technologies and lack of ownership of the technologies by the enterprise firms are some of the primary shortcomings of public cloud computing (Mahmood, 2011). Other considerations that organizations should address in choosing their approach to cloud computing include the security of the systems, their reliability, service levels, data privacy, and compliance with current technologies and regulation (Saboowala, 2013) (Vacca, 2012). This study will determine how public cloud computing fares in terms of these aspects, which will enable the determination of the feasibility of its applications in enterprise companies in Saudi Arabia. In this paper, the various models of cloud computing will be discussed at length, which will enable the identification of the strengths and shortcomings of public cloud computing in relation to other cloud computing models. In addition, the cloud computing needs of enterprise firms will be determined through an extensive literature review, which will create a framework for the data collection stage. Findings from this study will offer a solution for enterprise companies in Saudi Arabia on the suitability of cloud computing for their business practices in order to achieve a competitive edge, address challenges, and improve service delivery.

6

1.3 Research Objective

- To determine the extent to which adoption public cloud business applications by Saudi Arabian enterprise companies is feasible as a replacement for traditional business applications.

1.4 Research Questions

1.4.1 Main Research Question

- Is it feasible for enterprise companies in Saudi Arabia to switch from traditional business applications and use public cloud computing services for their day-to-day business operations?

1.4.2 Sub-Questions

q1. What factors in the Saudi Arabian environment affect the implementation of public cloud computing by enterprise firms in Saudi Arabia?

q2. What are the benefits and shortcomings of implementing public cloud computing technologies by enterprise firms in Saudi Arabia?

q3. How can enterprise companies in Saudi Arabia optimize the benefits of public cloud computing without succumbing to challenges in the environment and the shortcomings of public cloud computing?

1.5 Scope and Limitations of Study

1.5.1 Delimitations

Review of literature for this study will be limited to research done in relation to the applications, importance and other aspects of cloud computing, but the technical aspects of cloud computing will be excluded. For instance, the specific technologies required for implementation of cloud computing including hardware and software will be left out as this study will only focus on the managerial and the functional aspect of cloud computing implementation. While the literature review will not be limited in terms of the geographical region since cloud computing is a global phenomenon, the methodology aspect will be limited to a few companies within Saudi Arabia, which is the context for this study. Although a limited number of companies will be used for this study, the methodology will also not address the technical aspect of cloud computing implementation; only the aspects that address its feasibility will be addressed. Cloud computing occurs in multiple forms, but public cloud computing is the most common of all forms, which makes it the most feasible to assess due to information availability. In the case of private and other cloud computing approaches used by enterprise companies, available information may be limited as companies use cloud computing as part of their competitive strategy. Therefore, except for mentioning other computing approaches for comparison purposes, this study will be centered on public cloud computing.

1.5.2 Limitations

An effective research should have a sample that is representative of the population for purposes of generalization of research findings to the whole population, which can be a challenge, especially for qualitative studies. Since this study is qualitative in nature, the sample does not need to be representative as the primary purpose is to identify a general trend, but this is also a limitation since further study is required to account for all population parameters. Another limitation in regard to generalization and representativeness of the sample is the sample selection process, which is highly limiting since the selected companies depend on their willingness to participate. Since companies may use cloud computing as a strategy in achieving competitive advantage, the management of companies may be reluctant to divulge information about their knowledge management and information management strategies. In addition, the companies need to have implemented cloud computing for at least 5 years in order to have had experience and, therefore, knowledge on its feasibility. This inclusion requirement increases the limitations of this study since cloud computing is a fairly recent technological development that is in its early developmental phases. In the review of literature, the researcher will have challenges finding appropriate sources for use in this study since cloud computing is an emerging technology and not much research has been done on its application in the business environment.

1.6 Route Map to the Dissertation

In order to answer the research questions successfully and achieve the objectives of this study, the rest of the dissertation is organized into chapters with headings and subheadings around which ideas and concepts are organized. The chapters include literature review, data and methods, analysis and results, discussions and conclusions, references and appendices. The literature review includes a critical analysis of previous studies done on the topic of study, which serves to give a background and perspective to this study. The data and methods chapter includes the process through which both primary and secondary data were collected and consolidated before final analysis. In the analysis and results chapter, the findings of the procedures described in preceding chapters were analyzed in order to make sense of them and apply them in answering of research questions. The final chapter of the dissertation body was the discussion and conclusions chapter, which was used to relate the findings of this study to those of previous studies, which clarified the contribution of this study to the existing body of knowledge. Other topics in this dissertation are the references and appendices, which provide additional information for use together with the information contained in the main body of the dissertation.

CHAPTER 2: LITERATURE REVIEW

2.1 Organization of review

The literature review will discuss the emergence and adoption of cloud computing, especially in regard to its effect on the cost cutting, profitability and competitiveness of business enterprises. Then, the main approaches to cloud computing will be discussed, including a comparison of the strengths and shortcomings of each approach. Some of the aspects that will discussed in regard to various cloud computing deployment approaches include their effects on profitability and cost of doing business, and current adoption levels by enterprise firms, governments, individuals and other commercial and noncommercial entities. After that, the cloud computing will be discussed in regard to the cloud computing needs of various business sizes, forms and approaches, especially in regard to the unique benefits of the different applications of cloud computing. The final and most important theme for the literature review will involve discussion of the current state of cloud computing in Saudi Arabia in relation to the economic, cultural, environmental, technological and legal conditions.

2.2 Emergence and Adoption of Cloud Computing

The implications of cloud computing and its potential benefits cannot be missed by business entities, and KPMG determined in a 2012 studies that over 81% of the companies under review had either implemented cloud computing, or were evaluating and planning to incorporate cloud computing in their processes (Aerohive Networks, 2013). According to (Aerohive Networks, 2013, p. 2), organizations have realized the potential benefits of cloud computing including increased flexibility, scalability and agility of their business practices, which comes from the ability to adapt to changes in their workload without having to change their IT budgets significantly. Cloud computing enabled a business to outsource a considerable portion of technical duties, which frees employees to work on implementing and improving the company's core competencies (Hastings, 2009). By installing applications and hosting data in distant servers, the responsibility of owning complex technologies and ensuring the safety of company data is transferred to a third party with the capabilities and capacity to own and maintain the necessary infrastructure and knowledge (Hayes, 2008). In this regard, the development of cloud computing has enabled businesses to acquire the advanced technological functionality that would have otherwise be unachievable due to prohibitive costs of the necessary technologies. Since most of the innovation seems focused on cloud computing instead of conventional software implementations , the benefits of cloud computing will be enhanced with time and its shortcomings addressed, which will make it easier for business entities to decide the best cloud computing approach for their activities (Hayes, 2008, p. 9). For instance, due to network and processor virtualization, dependability of cloud computing in terms of fault

10

tolerance and real-time operations are difficult to achieve (Mullender, 2012), but with the current commitment in research and development of these technologies, these challenges will be addressed.

The US National Institute of Standards and Technology (NIST) is responsible for providing the guidelines on which implementation of cloud computing should be based, which include various recommendations and definitions as cited by (Ananthi, 2012, p. 1), (Bender, 2012, p. 2), and (ISACA, 2009, p. 6). According to NIST, cloud computing has five primary characteristics including measured service, rapid elasticity, resource pooling, broad network access and on-demand self-service, which are important in determining the cost effectiveness of migration from grid computing to cloud computing (Chen, et al., 2013). According to (Chen, et al., 2013), the compatibility of these characteristics of cloud computing with conventional computing has made the migration of data and functionality to cloud computing highly manageable and economical.

The on-demand self-service property of cloud computing allows for customers to acquire and utilize the service provider's resources with minimal human interaction, which not only frees human resources for other important tasks, but is also indispensable in cost cutting. The broad network access property of cloud computing should enable users to connect and use the resources of the cloud network using any device that has internet connection including laptops, smartphones, tablet computers, personal computers, PDAs and other mobile devices. The resource pooling property of cloud computing enables service providers to serve multiple customers using shared resources, whereby virtual and physical resources are assigned to customers according to demand but without the knowledge of the customers. At higher levels of abstraction, customers may be able to specify the processing, storage, memory, virtual machines and network bandwidths based on abstract identifiers like data center, region and country. The rapid elasticity property of cloud computing allows for rapid and elastic provisioning of resources and capabilities, usually automatically, such that they appear unlimited for customers to buy. The measured service property of cloud computing accounts for the ability of automatic control and optimization of active user accounts, processing, storage and bandwidth which allows for transparent control, monitoring and reporting of utilized service to the customer and service provider (Ananthi, 2012, p. 1) ; (Bender, 2012, p. 2); and (ISACA, 2009, p. 6). Based on the characteristics of cloud computing as provided by NIST, cloud computing shares similar characteristics with conventional computing, but the former allows for greater adaptability of resources to customer needs. In this regard, customers can export their computing needs including storage, processing and memory to the cloud in a cost-effective manner since the implementation and maintenance of cloud computing requires less resources in terms of time, finances and IT equipment in comparison to conventional computing (Chen, et al., 2013).

Although cloud computing continues to evolve and become easier and cheaper to adopt, (Brynjolfsson, et al., 2010) argue that the utility model of adoption is advantageous but the compatibility and ease of use for cloud computing may not achieve the levels observed in utilities like water and electricity. Nevertheless, compatibility and interoperability of cloud computing applications has been improving such that, by 2012, desktop computers, laptop computers, smartphones, tablets and eReaders were used at workplaces at percentages of 69, 63, 49, 24 and 5 percent respectively (McCourt, 2012, p. 70). Using these devices, cloud computing enables a user to access applications and data through a web browser to open and edit files that require the use of specialized software without having to buy and install such software. In addition, cloud computing allows for remote access of files, whereby a person can access a file through the Internet while at a different geographical location from the hard drive containing the file (Dixon, 2012, p. 36). According to (Dixon, 2012, p. 36), the most common examples of cloud computing applications include electronic mail accounts like Gmail, Outlook and Yahoo, and social network accounts like Facebook, LinkedIn and Twitter, which can be accessed using any Internet connected device. According to (Skiba, 2011, pp. 266-267), 37% of businesses, 34% of higher education institutions, 30% of healthcare institutions and 21% percent of small businesses use cloud applications like file storage, email, web conferencing, video conferencing and online earning. In 2011, the most common cloud computing services included Gmail, Google docs, Microsoft Live Meeting, WebEx and GoToMeeting at 34%, 29%, 29%, 28% and 24% respectively. According to (Marston, 2011, pp. 179-180), cloud computing has resulted in the emergence and growth of technology industry leading firms like IBM, Google, Microsoft, AT&T, Apache, EMC, Cisco, Amazon, SalesForce.com, Enomaly, CapGemini, Rightscale and Vordel (Marston, 2011, pp. 179-180). These companies have played the roles of innovators, enablers, technology providers or market players, which has increased the feasibility and availability of cloud computing services by end users.

According to (Ernst&Young, 2011), the availability, costs and usability of cloud computing services are dependent on multiple factors in the business environment, whereby each of these factors determine the ability of a customer to adopt and apply the cloud computing services. First, the business model adopted by a service provider determines the pricing of various cloud computing bundles, which ranges from free access to monthly and annual subscriptions. Second, how the service provider interacts with and manages strategic sourcing of resources determines the availability of services, costs and quality of services. Third, privacy of customer data and security is a matter of concern for both service providers and customers since pooling of resources presents the challenge of separating information and data from different customers (Smith, 2009, p. 67). Fourth, since cloud computing is a relatively new phenomenon, standardization of service delivery is yet to be universalized, which means products may not be of the expected standards, or may not be compatible with comparable services from competitors. Fifth, governments have yet to address the cloud computing comprehensively, especially in regard to intellectual property rights and copyright laws. Sixth, as opposed to grid computing where various IT tools have specific functions, cloud computing spans multiple departments and functions, which presents accounting challenges. Seventh, cloud computing operates in a globalized platform, which means that businesses and governments have to address the challenge of cross-border taxation for a service that cannot be fully quantified. Finally, the online hosting of cloud services makes it difficult for businesses to ascertain their compliance to international or local regulations prior to implementation.

In addition to security and privacy challenges, (Smith, 2009, p. 67) identified five more shortcomings in cloud computing that may hinder the benefits from cloud computing advantages such as cost cutting and scalability. Data hosting in foreign countries exposes the data hosted in the cloud to be subject to the laws of the hosting countries, which makes the data vulnerable to access by third parties. In addition, the performance of cloud applications fluctuate highly due to shared resources, which can make it difficult for one to work when a server or application is assigned to many people in the same neighborhood simultaneously. The complexity of cloud computing systems exposes them to complex bugs, which may result in loss of service for hours or days until the bug is fixed. Since cloud computing is still a recent computer technology implementation, standards have not yet been established to ensure cross compatibility, which means a company that embedded in one service may have difficulties switching a vendor. Although the resources of a cloud computing service provider seem to be unlimited, if all customers called on the services at the same time, the vendor may run out of resources, which may result in loss of service when customers need them the most.

Although cloud computing has multiple shortcomings, the most commonly identified is security (Reddy, 2011); (Saranya, et al., 2013) whereby vast resources have been invested in developing security features to protect the data and information about customers from unauthorized access. According to (Saranya, et al., 2013), the security challenge in cloud computing emerges from the difficulty in allowing for third party authentication without exposing customer information to unauthorized parties. In order to address these loopholes, service providers have implemented a layering system in which a Security as a Service layer used across Software, Platform and Infrastructure service layers (Reddy, 2011). Therefore, cloud computing has emerged as an important phenomenon if data management and received enthusiastic support, but its stability is challenged by security issues, dependability and stability.

2.3 Cloud Computing Approaches

Depending on the products offered by the service provider, cloud computing can be divided into three main cloud computing service models including Software as a Service (SaaS), Platform as a Service (PaaS) and Infrastructure as a Service (IaaS) (Ananthi, 2012, p. 1) ; (Bender, 2012, p. 2) ; (Hilley, 2009) ; (Hoefer, 2010) ; (Awad, 2011). Although it has not received widespread use, (Rimal, et al., 2009) also came up with a fourth model of cloud computing product type known as Hardware as a Service (HaaS). In the SaaS service model, software is available for on-demand distribution over the Internet, which is

13

centrally hosted for remote usage by customers and the service provider configures, updates and maintains it from a central location. Google Docs is an example of a SaaS application that is an online tool for creation and storage of basic information in documents that are accessible form any Internet-connected device. In the IaaS service model, the service provider, including Amazon EC2 and VITI provides software, hardware, facilities and expertise that allow users to install applications and use them until completion of their life cycles. In this regard, the IaaS service model acts as remote server that has an operating system and other resources, which enables the customer to install and use applications remotely. The PaaS service model was designed for developers, whereby a set of rules, tools guidelines like Microsoft Azure are available for developers when developing cloud applications. Although NIST does not describe a HaaS model, (Rimal, et al., 2009) point out that IT automation, hardware virtualization, and pricing and metering of hardware usage have made it possible for users to subscribe and use IT hardware or even entire data centers without having to build and manage them.

According to (Aerohive Networks, 2013, p. 2), the primary deployment models of cloud computing include public and private cloud computing, whereby the former is provided over the Internet and applications and infrastructures are hosted at the service provider's premises while the latter is provided locally with resources hosted in the customer's data center on a private platform. Implementation of technologies between the two approaches is similar in that hardware and processing power and virtualized and storage is shared, but sharing of resources is either public in public cloud computing or limited to a single organization in private cloud computing. In addition to public and private cloud computing, NIST recognizes 2 other models of cloud computing including community cloud and hybrid cloud computing (Bender, 2012, pp. 2-3). A community cloud is put in place and deployed for use by a limited community of users with shared interests and concerns including security requirements, mission, compliance, and policy considerations. A community cloud may be owned and hosted by one or more members of the community, or it may be outsourced from a third party (Bender, 2012, p. 3). A hybrid cloud is a cloud computing deployment approach in which a combination of any two or more cloud computing infrastructures including private, community or public cloud, are implemented together. In hybrid cloud computing, the cloud infrastructures remain as distinct units but are bound by proprietary or standardized technologies that enable for application and data portability (Bender, 2012, p. 3). The choice of a cloud computing approach by a customer depends on computing needs, available resources, and the strengths and shortcomings of each cloud computing implementation approach.

Cloud computing implementation models have both advantages and disadvantages, and a customer's choice is dependent on the IT priorities, budget and available options. Public cloud services are efficient and simple, low cost, require minimal time to adjust capacity based on changing requirements, have no maintenance costs or obligations, and no contracts are required, especially with the

14

pay-as-you-go model (Aerohive Networks, 2013, p. 3). The main disadvantages of public cloud computing include loss of control by the customer over resources, slow speed because processing is dependent on speed of Internet connection, renting from third party means that the investment capital of a business does not improve, and perceived weak security especially for users that deal with sensitive information (Aerohive Networks, 2013, p. 3). Private clouds allow for greater control over data, increased security and performance since they operate behind a firewall in an intranet, deeper compliance of data to HIPAA, PCI DSS and Sarbanes Oxley standards, highly customizable hardware, network and storage performance (Aerohive Networks, 2013, p. 3). Disadvantages of private cloud computing include performance ceiling due to hardware limitations, higher risk and cost due to hardware and software maintenance, and higher costs of acquiring, upgrading and maintaining hardware and software (Aerohive Networks, 2013, p. 3).

In view of the shortcomings of both public and private cloud computing deployment approaches, (Géczy, et al., 2012) recommend hybrid cloud computing since it acts as a middle ground in which benefits of both approaches can be optimized and their shortcomings suppressed. Some of the benefits that can be harnessed from hybrid cloud computing include a balanced approach to benefits and risks, efficient and faster adoption due to similarity to conventional outsourcing, and fast deployment of the public aspect of the hybrid cloud. In addition, hybrid cloud computing has other benefits like ease of use in adoption of ready-to-use private and public cloud solutions, transfer and elimination of costly third party cloud solutions to cut costs, timely and dynamic scaling of resources with change in demand, and ease of payment as users pay only for cloud services used. In spite of the far-reaching benefits of hybrid cloud computing over private and public cloud computing, (Géczy, et al., 2012) identified some shortcomings that may limit the benefits and usability of the hybrid cloud. Some of these shortcomings include potential risk elevation due to poor balance between the public and private aspects of the cloud, fragmented control and customization of data, applications and resources, and security risks in the public cloud. Other shortcomings of hybrid cloud computing include inconsistent access to data and services due to network connection fluctuations, the public cloud creates a liability risk as the service provider is not liable to losses, breaches and compromises, and remote hosting in the public cloud may put valuable company data in unprotected territories.

Although cloud computing has obvious benefits, there are challenges that users have to overcome in its implementations, which has caused some writers like (Chauhan, et al., 2012) to consider cloud computing a failure. These authors cite the dubious nature of data and services management in the cloud as the primary reason for concerns about privacy and security, which, in turn, could result in complete failure of cloud computing. The fears expressed by (Chauhan, et al., 2012) are justified, but their approach to writing off cloud computing as a failure is shortsighted since the concerned stakeholders are taking measures to address these shortcomings. In order to address the security issues facing cloud computing, (Albeshri & Caelli, 2010, p. 642) recommend minimal movement of data and process location, data and process deletion upon contract termination, continuity and resilience of service, integral and consistent naming services, and guaranteed absence of deliberate or accidental interruptions. In addition to data and process security, privacy is another issue of concern; especially since data verification and auditing in cloud computing is done by third party auditors. However, (Ananthi, 2012, p. 2) point out that systems are in place to enable verification of correctness of data in the cloud by a third party without having to retrieve the data. One such approach was recommended by (Attas & Batrafi, 2011) who stated recommended a three step verification approach in which the user does the digital signature part, the cloud server verifies the data for intrusions and manipulations, and the third party auditor verifies the server to confirm the presence or absence of data modification by the cloud server. According to (Bowers, 2011, pp. 48-49), an effective cloud computing approach to ensure data security should have application and data encryption, data validation during input and output, copy protection, and allow only authorized copying, forwarding and printing of data.

The level of investment and care taken by service providers in ensuring security and privacy of data held in the cloud is dependent on the sensitivity of such data and its value to its user. According to (Kalyvas, et al., 2013, p. 11), the level of criticality of service is dependent on the sensitivity level of the data in question. Low risk cloud computing is cloud computing approaches that use generally available data and non-mission critical software, and variable performance and outages are acceptable. Medium risk cloud computing includes services like web conferencing that uses data that is generally available but uses high service levels, and customer lead management tools like salesforce.com that use enterprise data that is non-confidential. High risk cloud computing requires has mission critical processes that utilize sensitive data, which necessitates careful evaluation to ensure optimization of benefits and mitigation of risks. These cloud computing risks can be classified into organizational risks, operational risks, technical risks and legal risks, which must be addressed by both service providers and their customers to ensure that cloud computing results in more benefits to users than it costs (Dutta, et al., 2013, pp. 41-42). Once the security and privacy risks have been addressed, users can then enjoy cloud computing benefits like including reduced costs, increased storage, high levels of automation, increased flexibility, more employee mobility, shift focus to core tasks by eliminating software and hardware updates, immediacy of implementation, scalability, resiliency and efficiency (Ananthi, 2012, p. 1); (ISACA, 2009, pp. 6-7). These benefits of cloud computing are enhanced by the fact that cloud computing can adapt to IT needs of a user on a minute-by-minute basis, upgrading to higher service requirements requires minimal investment, and cloud servers have greater computing server at a cost-friendly rate in comparison to conventional computing (Armbrust, et al., 2010, p. 52). The differences in implementation between conventional computing and cloud computing account for differences in economics of the two approaches since, in comparison, the former is more capital intensive, time consuming and relatively inflexible (Bayrak, et al., 2011). In order to ensure successful adoption of cloud computing and protection of the user's interests (Coutinho, 2012) recommended a comprehensive understanding of outstanding risks and service-level agreements. On the other hand, service providers can optimize the effectiveness or efficiency of their services through improvement of energy efficiency of cloud computing systems to minimize power consumption through the use of a power saving/sleep to reduce idle draw power, and consolidating tasks in an energy-conscious manner (Lee & Zomaya, 2010). Saving on power consumption by service providers should enable them to pass on the benefits to their customers, which results in reduced costs of cloud computing implementation for more widespread adoption.

2.4 Cloud Computing in Business

In business, cloud computing has the benefits that relate to improvements in finances and data management, whereby it enables a business entity to manage data more effectively at lesser costs in comparison to conventional banking. According to (Skiba, 2011, p. 267), one of the primary benefits of cloud computing is that it enables a business entity to minimize the costs of acquiring, deploying, upgrading and maintaining information technology hardware and software. These financial benefits of cloud computing are obtained by changing information technology expenses of small and medium-sized businesses from a capital expense to an operating expenses (Wessels, 2011). In the face of increasing globalization, the ability of different departments or strategic business units to operate in different geographical regions offers opportunities for cost cutting, time saving, market advantage and other factors that give a competitive edge. In this regard, cloud computing implementations like instant messaging, video conferencing, online data storage and email have multiple organizational benefits for small and medium-sized businesses (Wessels, 2011). According to (Leandro, et al., 2012) the economic benefits of cloud computing to businesses can be optimized when the effectiveness and efficiency of operations have been improved. One primary way of improving cloud computing implementation to result in financial benefits for businesses is by addressing security challenges through outsourcing of authorization and authentication mechanisms to trusted and independent third parties.

According to (Leimeister, et al., 2010), businesses can acquire and use cloud computing at different levels of the cloud computing implementation layers depending on the available resources, security needs, level of control and the technical requirements of the business processes. The layer of cloud software infrastructure is subdivided into computational resources (IaaS), storage (DaaS), and communications (CaaS). The implications of these cloud computing service layers are so far-reaching address many data collection, storage, processing and retrieval needs of a business, such that any business that does not consider the implementation of one or more cloud computing approach may face a competitive disadvantage (Plummer & Gartner, 2012).

The power, financial and time savings among other benefits of cloud computing make it suitable for use in various commercial and noncommercial case scenarios. For instance, for research activities that do not require specialist equipment and software, saving and managing data on the cloud could result in considerable savings for researchers (Chen, et al., 2010). However, many research studies require specialist hardware and software, (Chen, et al., 2010) recommended that, until more software becomes available on the cloud and the usage becomes more user friendly, researchers should use conventional computing as their primary computing method. Therefore, unless in studies where minimal specialist data analysis is required, researchers should use conventional computing for most tasks, but use cloud computing as a backup facility for their research data. In modern research that evolves rapidly and is highly dependent on the findings of others for one's study to be relevant, sharing information on the cloud is of paramount importance (Rosenthal, et al., 2010). This importance has been recognized by various research and standards bodies, such that specialist resources have been implemented for biomedical research including genetic and protein sequencing (Rosenthal, et al., 2010). Therefore, since cloud computing may not be applicable for all steps of the research process, research institutions should use a combination of offline data centers and online clouds to address all computing needs of the research process.

In commercial enterprises, cloud computing can be applied by small, medium and large enterprises, whereby the implementation is highly dependent on the specific needs of the enterprise in question. For large corporations, cloud computing may be implemented at a departmental level including the virtualization of accounting records to make them available for use by various company stakeholders (Awad, 2011). According to (Awad, 2011), cloud computing enables differentiated availability and accessibility of company information to various individuals and departments depending on their role in the company. Another approach to departmental virtualization is evident in healthcare institutions where patient results from different departments are posted in a private cloud for central access for diagnosis, treatment and billing purposes (Kharat, et al., 2012). On the other hand, institutional data can be posted to a public or community cloud for purposes of standardization, auditing and performance review. Therefore, large businesses usually require a hybrid cloud in which data availability is separated by sensitivity and necessity. Small and medium sized enterprises have common cloud computing needs, especially in regard to limitations in their budgets that would not allow for implementation of fully-fledged data centers for private cloud computing (DynaSis, 2011). According to (Karabek, 2011, p. 28), public cloud computing is beneficial for business enterprises in terms of short implementation cycles, low entry costs, low risk of obsolescence, customization, integration, reduced requirement to own IT resources, free resources to focus on core business, and enhanced collaboration and mobility. According to (Karabek, 2011, p. 29), small and medium sized enterprises prefer cloud computing services from local service providers because they offer individual, personal and flexible services.

According to (Hilley, 2009), cloud computing enables users to continuously adjust their IT capacity based on their needs, which enables them to minimize expenditure in comparison to having static data centers. Some cloud computing early adopters who obtained the benefits of cloud computing and can be used as examples for other business entities include New York Times, Washington Post, Defense Information Systems Agency (DISA), SmugMug, Eli Lily, Best Buy's Giftag, and Total Claims Capture & Control (TC3) (Hilley, 2009). New York Times managed to digitize its 1851 to 1922 historical papers using EC2 in an exercise that cost only $890 instead of a higher investment to buy a new server and over 3 months to digitize the content. Washington Post managed to convert into a searchable database over 17,000 pages of document images for documents released by the White House using only $144.62 within a day. Instead of spending $30,000 on servers and specialized software, DISA outsourced the software from Amazon Web Services at 10 cents per hour on service and $5 for software development. SmugMug, which is a Flickr-like photo hosting and sharing website saved $ 500,000 in disk drive costs by opting to outsource Amazon S3 at $23,000 monthly inclusive of storage, maintenance, cooling and power. Eli Lily, a leading pharmaceutical company, managed to reduce its server acquisition and deployment times from an average of 7 and a half weeks to about 3 minutes by using Amazon cloud services. These benefits of cloud computing to the business activities of an organization, together with energy savings and environmental conservation (Cubitt, et al., 2011), show that the benefits and implications of cloud computing are far-reaching.

Evidence from early adopters show that cloud computing is a phenomenon that could herald multiple benefits for both commercial and noncommercial entities, but implementers of cloud computing have to make some tradeoffs due to some shortcomings of cloud computing. According to (Hofmann & Woods, 2010), these tradeoffs include network limits and latencies, performance instability, difficulty in adjusting memory, storage and processing architecture, and lack of interoperability between cloud providers. According to (Science Magazine, 2010), some of these shortcomings can be overcome by avoiding the use of clouds as the primary source of storage, processing power and memory. However, this could require implementation of a local cloud, which would increase costs and negate the benefits of implementing cloud computing in a public cloud. Nevertheless, these shortcomings are being addressed with the evolution of cloud computing services, whereby the primary challenge that hinders businesses from enjoying the scalability, resilience, flexibility and other advantages of cloud computing is security (Kuyoro, et al., 2011).

Security issues are brought about by compliance to standards and governance, trust between the customer and service provider, service implementation architecture, customer identity and access management, data protection, software isolation, incident response and service availability (Jamil & Zaki, 2011) ; (Jansen & Grance, 2011). Although customers may not have the ability or capacity to address the security issues in services provided by service providers, they should ensure that the services have access control methods (Khan, 2012), and address the privacy needs of businesses (Schwartz, 2013). In addition, service providers should allow for remote checking of data integrity (Vimalraj & Manoj, 2009), especially through the use of third party systems for verification and auditing (Wang, et al., 2011). Once businesses can ensure that these issues have been addressed prior to implementation of cloud computing (Ryan & Loeffler, 2010), then cloud computing can work for the benefit of the businesses by giving them a competitive advantage (IBM, 2013)

2.5 Cloud Computing in Saudi Arabia

A country or region's level of economic development determines the extent to which residents can adopt the use of information technology tools in their businesses, especially due to the prohibitive costs of acquiring, maintaining, replacing and using information technology hardware and software. Cloud computing eliminates these expenses by consolidating the processing, storage and memory expenses into one usage bill for the user. Consequently, cloud computing puts all countries at par with developed countries in regards to the use of information technology in data management in business situations (Kshetri, 2010). In this respect, cloud computing can drive economic development as long as a country's laws and policies permit the hosting of data and data processing in remote locations. Even in cases where laws governing data management may not be compatible, service providers may modify their services to suit the target market, especially if such a market is significant to the market size and profitability of the providers. Therefore, cloud computing can enable countries worldwide to improve their development state to be at par with the most developed countries (Juster, 2008). Although Saudi Arabia may not be that badly off in terms of economic development, its economy needs to evolve beyond its current dependence on fossil oil in order to survive the exhaustion of the nonrenewable resource.

The primary issue differentiating users in Saudi Arabia and other countries in Middle East from the rest of the world is cultural factors, primarily because of the involvement of conservative philosophy in commerce, governance and other aspects of society. According to (Deng, et al., 2008), cultural background affects user satisfaction with computing in terms of content, format, accuracy, timeliness, and ease of use. However, the study by (Deng, et al., 2008) did not identify a conclusive result correlating culture and user satisfaction despite obvious evidence of a relationship between the two. Nevertheless, (Weber, 2011) determined factors in the global platform that may limit accessibility of cloud computing to businesses in Saudi Arabia. First, individual and family privacy are important issues in Middle East, which may limit access to resources since usage of cloud computing tools provided by multinational corporations require divulging personal information to unknown entities. In addition, businesses in Saudi Arabia may not trust western companies enough to post their business information online because of differences in data management policies with the western world. Second, in comparison to the western

20

market, Middle East market is fairly limited, and corporations in United States and Europe may be unwilling to invest in technical support and bug fixes, especially if those bugs and the needed technical support is specific to Middle East. Third, the technological development in Saudi Arabia may be hindered because businesses in Saudi Arabia will use terminals with limited functionality while all the storage, memory and processing power is located in mainframes owned by multinationals. Fourth, in order to subsidize the costs of some cloud computing services, content from external websites is advertised within the product. The content of these advertisements may not adhere to the conservative philosophy, which makes use of the services in Saudi Arabia either ethically wrong or illegal. Fifth, although businesses in Saudi Arabia have different computing needs in comparison to their western counterparts, the flexibility of cloud computing in terms of architecture is limited such that businesses would have to use what is provided by Google, IBM, Amazon, Microsoft and other multinationals. The best way to avoid overdependence on multinationals is by either using local service providers or by avoiding the use of cloud computing, which would be counterproductive.

In view of the challenges facing the use of cloud computing in Saudi Arabia, potential cloud computing customers should invest their time to familiarize with and decide on the outsourcing decision, vendor selection, service-level agreement and other issues that improve the feasibility of adoption of cloud computing (Yigitbasioglu, et al., 2013). Security is the main concern in implementing cloud computing, whereby users should identify a service provider that offers the most secure cloud computing services with minimal effects on performance. In addition, although cloud computing is so recent that few policies address privacy, anonymity, security, telecommunications capacity, reliability, government surveillance, liability issues, a business the effects of Saudi Arabian policy on these issues before adoption (Zamani, et al., 2011). In many cases, the adoption of cloud computing in Saudi Arabia is similar to adoption in other countries worldwide, but the role of data governance structure and cultural issues must be studied in order to determine the feasibility of adoption.

2.6 Conclusion

The major themes in this literature review show that cloud computing results in reduced costs of information technology use in business, especially by changing capital investment to a running cost. Cloud computing gives businesses a high level of flexibility and versatility due to the high performance and low maintenance nature of cloud computing services. In addition, cloud computing results in time and financial savings as the high level of scalability of memory, storage and processing enables a company to minimize the time required to complete a task from several months to a day or less. Despite these advantages of cloud computing, remote hosting of data and processing power results in dependability, privacy, security and other issues that limit the benefits of cloud computing. However, with continued development of cloud computing, most of these shortcomings are being addressed, and the primary presenting issues involve the security and privacy of sensitive business and personal data. In Saudi Arabia, the challenges faced by users and service providers go beyond the generic security and privacy issues primarily due to the role played by culture and religion in the personal and commercial aspects of life in the country. For instance, personal and family privacy in Saudi Arabia is an issue of concern, which causes people to be reluctant to divulge the information required to use cloud computing services. Disparities in service provision between various regions could also affect the adoption and feasibility of cloud computing in enterprise institutions in Saudi Arabia. Despite the availability of extensive information about cloud computing, no comprehensive empirical studies have been done to determine the role of culture, politics and economy on the adoption of cloud computing. Therefore, the literature review for this study was done on the assumption that the obvious advantages of cloud computing are enough to encourage its adoption. Even after conducting this study, these factors will not be studied fully since only business enterprises in Saudi Arabia will be studied and no comparisons to the rest of the world will be done. Since study in this and related topics is in its early stages, the objective of this study will be to determine general trends in adoption of cloud computing in Saudi Arabia to act as a baseline for future studies. In this regard, a semi-structured questionnaire is the most appropriate data collection tool for this survey.

CHAPTER 3: DATA AND METHODS

3.1 Most promising methodological approach

Due to the recent emergence of cloud computing as a recent information technology phenomenon, few empirical studies have been done to determine the feasibility, importance and other aspects of cloud computing. In addition, cloud computing adoption is only deep-rooted in the west, which means that meaningful quantitative data on cloud computing is only available in North America, Europe and other developed regions. As seen in multiple studies in the literature review, the most appropriate approach to collecting data for this study is through a survey using either a fully structured or semi-structured questionnaire. The survey, especially in Saudi Arabia, should be primarily done to collect qualitative data, which will offer an overview of trends on the success and feasibility of cloud computing in enterprise firms in Saudi Arabia.

3.2 Research Design and Method

This study was a combination of primary and secondary research, whereby secondary research was done from online databases, and primary research was done through interviews on a select number of respondents. Secondary research, which is presented in chapter 2 of this report, was used to create a background on the current state of knowledge in terms of implementation and factors that determine the success of public cloud computing. In this chapter, the primary research aspect of this study is presented, which was used to determine the extent to which the factors identified in the literature review affect enterprise companies in Saudi Arabia. Data collected in the primary research was qualitative, whereby a semi-structured questionnaire was used as a guide in interviewing the study respondents. In order to confirm the validity of the collected data, triangulation was done using the approaches to data and methodological triangulation as described by (Guion, et al., 2011). On one hand, data triangulation involved data collection from multiple participants including members of managements from enterprise companies in Saudi Arabia. On the other hand, methodological triangulation for the study involved collection of data from both primary and secondary sources.

3.3 Research Participants Recruitment Method

Enterprise companies in Saudi Arabia were identified in order to come up with a convenient sample based on the requirements of this study including the existence of the company for over 5 years and use of information technology tools in at least some of their business functions and processes. Research invitations, including a consent form and a plain language statement as attached in appendices A and B, were sent to 15 companies with the hope of receiving a positive response from at least 10 of the chosen enterprise companies. The consent form was aimed at getting the potential respondents to participate in this study out of their own free will in full understanding of the implications of their

23

participation in terms of privacy and security concerns. Prior to the delivery of these documents, calls were made to these small to medium-sized enterprise companies to request their participation in the survey. Once the company representatives expressed interest in participating in this study, they were informed that the researcher would be contacting them soon for further collaboration. Companies chosen for participation in this study included small (0 to 49 employees) and medium (50 to 249 employees) sized enterprise companies (Archives, 2006). By identifying small to medium enterprises, this study was aimed at showing that the benefits of cloud computing go beyond casual use by individuals and large-scale use by big corporations, but is also useful to organizations that have minimal information technology needs.

3.4 Research Participant Recruitment Criteria

In order to ensure the validity and applicability of their responses to this study, various criteria were used as bases for participant recruitment. First, the enterprise company of interest must have been in operation for 10 years or more to ensure that the company had worked without cloud computing but had implemented cloud computing to improve its processes and functions. Second, companies chosen for the study had IT departments that dealt with outsourcing of information technology services, implementation of cloud computing and maintenance of the companies' IT equipment. Third, the participants interviewed for the study had worked for their company for at least 5 years to ensure familiarity with the activities and developments in the company. Fourth, the participants had either worked in the IT departments of their respective companies or had knowledge about cloud computing implementation, and could connect their employers' financial performance with their IT activities. Based on the responses, the sample used for this study consisted of junior and senior IT managers, and experienced employees who had insights in relation to the topic of question.

3.5 Interviews

Interviews were conducted from January 19, 2014 to January 23, 2014 on individuals from 10 companies that responded positively to the request for participation. Each company provided 3 or 4 of their personnel, and the total participants for the interviews were 34 since 4 of the companies provided 4 participants for the study. Instead of the proposed focus group interviews, participants from each company were interviewed separately with each group being interviewed in either the morning hours or afternoon hours during the data collection week. While most of the discussion during the interview will be open-ended, the semi-structured questionnaire acted as a guide to focus the study to the discussion of level of awareness and implementation of public cloud computing, and the challenges faced in using current systems. Ethically, neither the participant's personal information nor the identities of their companies recorded, companies were coded as company 1 through to 10 as shown in appendix C. By so doing, none of the research findings of this study could be traced back to the originating source, which ensured a blind data collection and analysis process. In addition, the security of participants and data integrity was ensured by limiting access to research findings to only the researcher in line with ethical expectations of doing research.

3.6 Ethical Issues

Since the abovementioned part of this dissertation involved human subjects and company information that should be kept confidential for competition purposes, several measures had to be taken to protect the respondents and the companies they represented. For instance, the consent form included a statement of privacy, whereby companies, their employees and their responses in the study can be identified only by the researcher. In addition, as an additional means to protect the information, companies were coded in numbers 1 to 10, which meant that access to the information by unauthorized persons would not result in a connection between the collected data and the companies from which it was collected. As a further protection layer for the respondents, study participants were free to terminate their participation in the study whenever they had any misgivings about the study. Finally, no personal information was collected from respondents, and information that could affect a firm's position and performance in the market was avoided.

3.7 Literature Search

As mentioned above, the literature review is a central part of this study, whereby an extensive search was done in online databases in order to determine the current level of knowledge in the topic of study. Keywords related to the topic of interest in this study were used to search both academic and non-academic databases for literature that would provide insights on the role public cloud computing in the modern-day business environment. With the findings of the literature review as a background, the results of the interviews will be analyzed and reviewed to achieve the study objectives by answering the research questions. Regardless of direct reference in the discussion of research results, the results of literature review are always inferred in the discussion, whereby any conclusions are based on the research findings of both the primary and secondary research aspects of this study.

3.8 Analysis

The data collected in the interviews for this study was limited in both variability and amount, which made a manual data analysis the most appropriate approach. Through a theoretical conceptualization approach, the variables that affect the feasibility of implementation of public cloud computing by enterprise companies in Saudi Arabia were identified. Once the respondents provided their views, experience and perceptions of cloud computing, their views on implementation of recommendations to improve feasibility of cloud computing were also collected. Based on the dependent and independent variables of this study, the analysis done on the findings of this study were mainly descriptive in nature, whereby tables and summaries were used to make sense of the research findings. After analysis of study results, the findings of this study provided a clear guideline on successful implementation of cloud computing by enterprise companies in Saudi Arabia.

CHAPTER 4: ANALYSIS AND RESULTS

4.1 Data Analysis

The theoretical basis of this study is that cloud computing entails hosting of storage, processing power and memory in a remote location instead of the local hosting of conventional computing. Due to its recent emergence and the nature of operations in cloud computing, public cloud computing has various strengths and shortcomings as identified in the literature review. In order for implementation of cloud computing by enterprise companies in Saudi Arabia to be feasible, the strengths of cloud computing implementation must outweigh its shortcomings. In this regard, this analysis aimed at identifying ideas, themes, trends and categories in relation to the topic of study. For instance, the strengths and shortcomings of cloud computing were identified from the response provided by study respondents. In addition, the factors in the Saudi Arabian business environment that affect the feasibility of cloud computing were identified. As shown in the results and analysis in this chapter, and in the discussion in the next chapter, most of the findings in his study confirmed the findings of previous studies as identified and discussed in the literature review chapter. Moreover, possible solutions to cloud computing shortcomings and environmental challenges were identified and proposed to study respondents for their feedback on applicability. In spite of the common findings between previous studies and this one, the results of this study show that the factors determining approaches to cloud computing implementation are highly dependent on cultural, geographical, economic and other country-specific factors. For instance, the cloud computing systems that have been highly successful in the western world must be modified to fit into the society in Saudi Arabia due to differences in perceptions among the local populations.

4.2 Results

4.2.1 Factors in Saudi environment that affect cloud computing implementation

Factor	Details
Control	Slow adoption
	Tight control by IT departments and IT individuals
Economic	High oil-based income and economic growth
Social	Culture based on conservative philosophy
	Family and personal privacy concerns
Technological	Deregulation has resulted in widespread use of personal computers
	Ecommerce, electronics and electrical markets are rapidly growing
Legal	Data Compliance guides
	Type of information & Type of business
	Jurisdiction
	Localization (Arabic language)

Based on the table above, the respondents show that there is increase in the adoption of Public Cloud in Saudi Arabia, but this has been happening at a very slow rate over the past few years due to hesitation by organizations to adopt the emerging approach to technology implementation. However, organizations in Saudi Arabia are striving to improve business processes, show values, and transform the business, which in turn gives them chance to evaluate their current practices with cloud technologies. AS mentioned earlier, the need to implement cloud computing arises from the necessity brought about by the opportunity of increasing effectiveness, enhancing efficiency, cutting costs, and increasing revenue and profitability (Aerohive Networks, 2013, p. 2). Although the tendency in amongst Saudi companies is to maintain full control on all IT operations locally and on premise, cloud computing is gaining better priority status within the kingdom. In addition, the table shows that the oil-based economy of Saudi Arabia has the required resources put in place to have an IT infrastructure to access high-speed Internet connection within the kingdom. In this regard, companies in Saudi Arabia cannot blamed for poor infrastructure or failure to implement public cloud computing in an attempt to improve their business activities. Moreover, the table shows that having conservative-based cultural philosophy in which family and personal values have resulted in being wary of their privacy more than many other countries, where perceived awareness about cloud computing also plays a major role. Therefore companies and individuals are more reluctant to put their personal and corporate information online on to data storages for processing and retrieval services (Deng, Doll, Al-Gahtani, Larsen, Pearson, & & Raghunathan, 2008). This reluctance to post personal and corporate information online was seen to be caused by concerns about privacy and security of information, whereby parties are usually worried that their confidential and, sometimes, sensitive information may be exposed to unauthorized parties. Furthermore, the table shows that market deregulation of the computer and computer accessories has resulted in the growth of the computer electronics markets including mobile devices that has resulted in increased accessibility and use of web services and public cloud services. Finally, the table above also shows that the legal system in Saudi Arabia for data governance is not clearly defined, thus putting pressure on local companies to define and adhere to specific guidelines in handling their data in both online and offline locations. By doing so companies have to limit the content of the information shared on the cloud to further avoid antagonizing the government and local agencies (Zamani, Akhtar, & & Ahmad, 2011). Also, since Arabic language is the official language used by government and all official transactions across the kingdom, it was noted by respondents that localization is not provided by all cloud providers this will affect or limit the choices to use of this technology in certain industries to less service providers.

4.2.2 Cloud computing services implemented by enterprise companies in Saudi Arabia

Service	Examples
Office Suites	Google Docs, Microsoft Office, QuickBooks
Storage	Skydrive, Dropbox, Google Drive, Box, SugarSync
IT management	Service-Now, BMC Remedy Express, ManageEngine - IT Enterprise management
Messaging	Office 365, Gmail, Outlook, iCloud Mail, Yahoo
Infrastructure	Amazon (AWS), Microsoft Azure
Productivity	OfficeTime, Sage One, Adobe FormsCentral, DocuSign Pro, Office 365, Adobe Connect, Gliffy
CRM	Salesforce.com
Finance	Quicken, TurboTax, Abukai, QuickBooks, FreshBooks
Project management	Zoho, intuit
Database	QuickBase , Oracle Public Cloud

As shown in the table above, software as a platform is the most common service model of cloud computing, whereby most companies are not even aware of the Infrastructure as a Service, Hardware as a Service and Platform as a Service, which are discussed in depth in the literature review. These findings show that cloud computing in Saudi Arabia, especially in business enterprises, is in its early stages of implementation where companies are just learning about the merits of hosting their software, storage and processing power in a remote location. In spite of this, cloud computing in Saudi Arabia seem to have gotten quite a start and will soon advance to other forms of cloud computing, which will include complex software implementations before adopting other service models.

Online office suites are used for creating and managing simple office documents like spreadsheets, presentations, forms, drawings and text documents that are required for communication, record keeping, and other forms of information storage, processing and retrieval. As shown in the table above, some of the online office tools identified by study of the respondents include Google Docs, Microsoft Office, and Quickbooks. In addition, the table above also shows the online storage services where companies store their data remotely for retrieval using different devices from multiple locations, this is convenient for file shares, disaster recovery and backup purpose. Some of the online storage services identified by Saudi Arabian businesses include dropbox, Skydrive (now known as Onedrive), Google Drive, Box and SugarSync. By adopting these services, enterprise companies in Saudi Arabia are in the process of recognizing the benefits of cloud computing like flexibility, scalability and cost cutting, but have not yet managed to harness the full potential of the new approach to technology implementation (Wessels, 2011).

In addition to storing and managing their documents, companies need to maintain their IT Service Management processes. Tools such as Service-Now, BMC remedy express, ManageEngine- IT Enterprise management are identified by respondents which help companies to manage the life cycle of an IT service processes such as Service Level Management helping in recording, managing and controlling of any change in an IT Service. Besides, the Messaging services in the cloud is taking wide acceptance by the respondents whereby email mass storage and high availability is offered, it is observed that office365 provided by Microsoft is broadly considered in the IT plan of the respondents of this study. These online tools are more complex than online document processing tools, which shows that, although most companies in the Saudi Arabian environment have just started in their cloud computing implementation, some of them have taken advantage of specialized software that is hosted in remote servers and does not require high investments in hardware.

On the infrastructure side, IT hardware resources including memory, storage, processing power for customer specific needs and software environments building whereby the companies in the study were observed to use Amazon Services (AWS) and Microsoft Azure for this purpose. Another class of cloud computing tools that were identified in this study include online tools that are used for productivity purposes, like conversion of documents, collaborative editing and appending of digital signatures to documents. Some of the productivity tools used by Saudi Arabian companies include OfficeTime, Sage One, Adobe FormCentral, DocuSign Pro, Microsoft Office 365, Adobe Connect and Gliffy. Also, Customer Relationship Management CRM applications for Sales and Marketing departments offered in the Cloud such as salesforce.com are commonly known for most of the respondents and by their respective sales operations that are geographically distributed.

30

On the finance side, many respondents are using cloud based financial tools to manage their personal financials including investment portfolio, bank transactions, cost tracking, spending, income and expenses, and plan for retirement. These tools are mostly used for personal purpose and only few companies are using it because of the culture of the data sensitivity at the enterprise level. Other cloud-based software identified is project management to manage the project life cycle including time sheet, scheduling, resource planning, tasks and milestones. Some of tools identified are zoho and intuit. Lastly, database systems that include QuickBase and Oracle Public Cloud are being assessed and considered by the respondents.

Therefore, although preliminary findings show that cloud computing in Saudi Arabia is in its early stages of implementation and enterprise companies are implementing the simplest cloud computing tools first, closer scrutiny shows signs of progress towards more complex and specialized applications. In this regard, as mentioned in the literature review, cloud computing in Saudi Arabia may face challenges due to security and privacy concerns, but the rate of implementation has been steadily growing, albeit at a slower than expected rate. With time, cloud computing in Saudi Arabia will move from one in that is dominated by Software as a Platform service model to one in which service models like Infrastructure as a Service, Hardware as a Service and Platform as a Service are commonly implemented.

4.2.3 Benefits of Cloud Computing

Factor	Details
User friendly	Less technical skills, scalability, cost saving
Time	Higher processing power, easy scalability, telecommuting
Finances	IT equipment costs, cut cost, time saving
Collaboration	Geographical location, process simplification, consultation, feedback
Redundancy	Use of cloud storage as a backup
Integration	Cross cloud integration architecture

The table above shows some of the benefits derived from usage of cloud computing, especially in comparison to conventional computing, which goes on to show the extent to which implementation of cloud computing may be beneficial to users relative to conventional computing. Some of the benefits identified in this case include ease of use, time convenience, cost friendliness, multiple simultaneous usage, protection from data loss, and integration with other cloud computing offerings. Ease of use, which results from user-friendly design, ensures that cloud computing services can be used easily even by employees who do not have any technical skills. This plays a big role where training of staff is reduced, resulting in time and cost reduction when it comes to comparing with traditional computing. Also, it is identified that cloud computing gives companies the flexibility to scale up or down as when needed at much lower cost. This is again costly and time consuming in traditional computing. Moreover, benefits identified by respondents for their use of cloud computing services include time saving, collaboration with others from multiple locations, and redundancy purposes. By saving time for companies, cloud computing frees a lot of time for organizations that can be devoted to other activities that may benefit the companies in terms of their financial performance, market share and brand equity. In addition, cloud computing helps companies to cut expenses through enabling employees to telecommute and lowering the cost of IT equipment, which enables companies to utilize their financial resources to achieve more. Moreover, cloud computing gives companies the capacity to have employees collaborating from different geographical locations, which saves time, simplifies processes, and enhances communication within the company hierarchy for consultation and feedback purposes.

The data saved on the cloud from a particular geographical location can be accessed immediately from another location. For example, you could upload a file from Jeddah, Saudi Arabia on to a well-known cloud tool such as 'Dropbox', and you can almost instantly access it through a web-enabled mobile or any device from USA, Germany, United Kingdom, China, or Japan saving much time and cost. In addition, the data stored in the cloud can be copied to several personal computers and mobile devices, and the information is updated automatically after editing either on the web or from any of the connected devices. This connectedness has the advantage of reducing the necessity to continually copy one's documents after editing, or having to back up a file repeatedly to avoid loss of information. Finally, the table above shows that companies identified redundancy as one of the roles of public cloud computing services, whereby copies of important documents are stored in online locations in order to prevent the loss of these documents in case of a hardware or software failure. Another benefit is noted by the respondents that cloud based applications can be integrated with other cloud applications or local applications depends on the architecture using web services. Integration between cloud and local applications ensures that both cloud users and local users can collaborate seamlessly, thus saving time and finances that may be required to keep multiple systems updated.

4.2.4 Issues raised

Issue	Details
Security	Compared to private computing, cloud computing exposes stored data, infrastructure and other important services to unauthorized access
Privacy	In order to access cloud computing services, identifying information has to be provided to the service provider
Stability	Outages and fluctuations of service
Data ownership	Data stored in the cloud may be accessible to third parties, which makes limiting of usage impossible , SLA governance
Ambiguity	Crowdsourcing, crowd funding, cloud printing, cloud manufacturing
Dependency	Internet availability, locations coverage

Based on previous studies and the findings of this study, cloud computing is a highly beneficial tool for enterprise companies, which is helpful in cutting costs, increasing effectiveness and efficiency, and increasing revenue. Despite the obvious advantages of public cloud computing to business processes, functions and structures, the study respondents identified several issues of concern that may inhibit the usability and efficiency of public computing tools. First, public cloud computing entails using third party tools to process store and manage one's information, which may expose the said information to unauthorized parties and compromise a company's activities. In case unauthorized parties access this information, individuals may be exposed to the risk of cyber crimes, and companies may lose their competitive edge as important company information may be sold to competitors. Second, it may be difficult to prevent information from being tracked back to the original source since identifying information has to be provided to the service provider, which means that company, family and individual information may be exposed to security risks. Third, due to fluctuations in Internet connections and other factors that affect access to the World Wide Web, public cloud computing services frequently experience instability in terms of service speed and availability. Also, planned and unplanned outages if not correctly defined between parties in an SLA's can also hamper the business and the availability of the service. Fourth, public cloud computing, and the accessibility of data in public clouds to anyone with an Internet connection may compromise the ownership of information that may compromise a company's competitive edge, especially if competitors can access the said information. In addition, some information stored in the cloud may involve important strategic plans, patent information and other confidential documents that may even result to closure of an organization if accessed by parties with ill intentions. Fifth, data processing, transfer, storage and retrieval services available through the internet are ambiguously classified, whereby companies may not be clear if they are using crowd sourcing, crowd funding, cloud printing or cloud manufacturing. In this regard, information from research done globally

33

may indicate an increase in use of cloud computing for commercial purposes, but in real sense the numbers may represent a lack of understanding of cloud computing concepts among respondents. Finally, as cloud computing highly depends on Internet connection, access to companies' files or application on the cloud will also depend on the kind of connection the company has, is it fast, reliable and reasonably priced. Besides, in certain remote locations within Saudi Arabia, Internet infrastructure is not yet established and this could be a cause of concern for the related industries.

4.2.5 Acceptability of recommendations

Recommendation	Acceptability
Outsourcing from local providers	High
Limited sharing of sensitive documents or data	High
Gradual implementation to mitigate possibility of total failure	High
Using a service provider with a proven record	Medium
Encryption of stored information using security protocols by service provider	Medium
Removal of identifying and sensitive information before storage	Low
Using services from multiple providers for redundancy purposes	Low

In anticipation to solving the challenges faced by Saudi Arabian companies in implementing public cloud computing, several recommendations, as shown in the table above, were offered to respondents in an attempt to determine their level of acceptability. The extent to which the respondents accepted a recommendation depended on their willingness to take a risk, their understanding of the concepts in question, and the need for a service within the existing cloud computing infrastructure. Outsourcing the cloud computing services from local service providers was highly acceptable since it enables companies to limit access to company information only to locally used companies. Respondents prefer the Cloud Service provider to have a local presence, making it easier for them to interact during high priority activities and critical project phases. Also, this also takes care of data protection and compliance guidelines, since data will be within the country. In addition, the recommendation for limited sharing of sensitive company information in order to reduce the risk of access by unauthorized parties was highly acceptable, whereby sensitive information is only stored and processed in localized systems rather than in the cloud. The classification of the data sensitivity varies from business to business. For instance, financials data are classified to most of the respondents as sensitive data and cannot be made fully available outside the country, while data related to manufacturing or sales can be compromised and stored in the cloud outside the country. Moreover, in order to prevent complete failure of information systems and total loss of company data, the respondents were highly accepting to the idea of gradual implementation of cloud computing. Gradual implementation also assists in building internal knowledge base, in order to provide required support and obtain critical users experience information, this enables IT support staff to answer the questions and resolve issues in timely manner.

Other recommendations, including using service providers with proven performance records, high customer satisfaction, minimal downtime, and maximum uptime were accepted by many of the respondents. By using service providers who already have proven performance records and product quality, enterprise companies will greatly reduce the risk that accompanies using the services of a service provider who does not have much market experience. In addition, experienced service providers are more likely to have the infrastructure required to ensure uninterrupted and secure services, especially since they have had the time to study the market and come up with appropriate solutions for any challenges. Moreover, the recommendation to use of data encryption methods as means to respondents of predicting future performance of cloud computing services and ensuring only authorized access respectively. Although removal of identifying information prior to storage of data in the cloud and use of multiple providers for redundancy are sound recommendations for cloud computing, few of the respondents considered them acceptable. This means that making data untraceable back to the company and backing up using multiple providers are not priorities for companies in Saudi Arabia. In spite of these findings about the extent of acceptability of recommendations, continuous research is required in order to adapt cloud computing services to the evolving needs of enterprise companies in Saudi Arabia.

CHAPTER 5: DISCUSSIONS AND CONCLUSIONS

5.1 Findings Summary

All the Saudi Arabian enterprise companies in the sample agreed in terms of the value of cloud computing to their business practices, whereby effects on time saving, finances, collaboration and data redundancy were discussed at length. Time savings due to cloud computing are evident in cloud computing characteristics like high processing power and ease of scalability. For instance, respondents observed that is required less time to implement cloud computing in comparison to conventional computing. In addition, in contrast with conventional computing that limits movement of employees as they have to work at specific workstations, cloud computing allows for timesaving practices like telecommuting. Telecommuting is convenient for employees and results in savings in terms of time and money for their employer, which in turn reduces the cost of production that increases a company's profitability without increasing the costs of products and services. Cloud computing only requires a low-powered or low-end devices to access the cloud network, which means that costs on IT equipment are considerably reduced than if the company had to host and process its data locally. Other cost savings due to cloud computing result from the ability to outsource some non-core services to service providers and leaves the organization to focus on its core competencies and central tasks. By focusing only on the important tasks in the production process, cloud computing enables organizations to innovate faster and provide their customers with products that offer the best value for their money.

Study respondents identified issues that affect the implementation of cloud computing, whereby most of these issues were identified in the literature review as the primary shortcomings of cloud computing implementation. In comparison to conventional computing, public cloud computing exposes infrastructure, stored data and other important services to unauthorized access. In addition, the privacy of businesses, families and individuals may be compromised as users are supposed to provide identifying information to the service provider before using the cloud computing services. The stability of cloud computing services in terms of outages and fluctuations was also a matter of concern, whereby the services may be inaccessible or slow at a time of most need. The limited offering of cloud localization by enabling Arabic language was another matter of concern by the respondents. Due to differences in intellectual property laws in different jurisdictions, ownership of data stored in the cloud is a cause of concern as data stored in the cloud may be accessible to unauthorized persons depending on differences in data protection laws. The definition of cloud computing was also an important issue raised by the respondents, especially due to the lack of clear definitions and differences between cloud terms. In this regard, many of the companies did not have a clear cloud computing strategy despite using cloud computing for day-to-day business activities. Despite these shortcomings of cloud computing,

36

implementing of cloud computing and making changes to cloud adoption is a relatively easy process for small to medium size enterprise companies in Saudi Arabia.

Also, after observing the challenges facing implementation of cloud computing in small and medium sized enterprise companies in Saudi Arabia, several solutions were proposed based on the findings of the literature review and the views of participants collected. In order to counter the challenge of data protection in different jurisdictions, a recommendation to seek cloud computing services from local service providers was proposed. Using local service providers was unanimously accepted, but respondents claimed that local service providers may either have less than ideal services and efficiency, and others may be outsourcing from the companies the respondents wanted to avoid. Since it is impossible to determine the location of data hosting in a cloud computing setting, a proposal to share only non-sensitive documents was recommended. Sharing generic information that would not make sense out-of-context was accepted as the ideal approach to dealing with security and privacy issues, especially in regard to information that may affect the wellbeing of the company's business. Using a service provider with a proven record in terms of encryption of customer data and applications, and removal of identifying and sensitive information before data storage, was accepted as one way to reduce the risk. All respondents agreed that cloud computing should be implemented gradually from general tasks towards more specific tasks to give the company time to adjust its processes to align to new computing methods. Gradual implementation was unanimously accepted as a means to select the most suitable service providers since most participants agreed that managing the services from multiple providers was tasking.

In addition, most service providers are based in the West, and companies have to identify a service provider that tailors its products to suit the market in Saudi Arabia. This poses a challenge to the implementation process especially due to cultural differences between the two regions, which ultimately results in different business ethics and perceptions of socially acceptable and unacceptable behavior. However, most multinational service providers have managed to tailor their products to suit the needs of different geographical regions, and, although a locally-based company would be able to address all challenges, using the services of reputable multinationals addresses the most common challenges. Therefore, implementation of public cloud computing in Saudi Arabia is feasible as long as companies select a service provider with a positive reputation, limit posting of sensitive information to the cloud server, and implement cloud computing gradually to avert the possibility of complete failure. In addition, cloud computing by enterprise companies is sustainable in the long term if companies can keep adjusting their cloud computing implementations depending on their existing needs and improvements in cloud computing technologies. Furthermore, companies should always be watchful of the activities of their service providers in order to protect their information from theft and loss, which can be done by taking appropriate measures like switching to a better service provider.

5.2 Theoretical and Practical Implications

Theoretically, all cloud computing services are available to Saudi business entities, especially since there are no possible cultural, economic, social, political or legal factors that cold prevent businesses from implementing and taking advantage of cloud computing services. Saudi Arabia is ideal for implementation of cloud computing, especially as efforts are made to diversify the high oil-based economy through privatization and opening of economic cities, and also in regard to availability and stability of the infrastructure required to adopt the less demanding public cloud computing instead of other cloud computing implementation models. In addition, the resources required to implement the SaaS model of public cloud computing are easily available for both small and medium-sized businesses since cloud computing requires low investments in consumer-end hardware because the most challenging processing and storage tasks are handled by the server. However, the environment in which these business entities implement their cloud computing strategies limit the extent to which small and medium-sized companies in Saudi Arabia can enjoy the benefits of public cloud computing. The practical implications of the findings of this study, therefore, show that the effects of cultural aspects on the Saudi Arabian conservative environment and legal system result in prohibition of some practices that are common with cloud computing users in other geographical regions. For instance, with the requirement to present identifying information to service provider for registration and security purposes, some companies in Saudi Arabia may be reluctant to use cloud computing services since they operate in a cultural environment where family, personal and business privacy is highly valued. Therefore, although companies in Saudi Arabia have endless opportunities opened up by cloud computing, the environment in which they trade can limit the extent to which they trade can implement public cloud computing for their business activities.

5.3 Limitations

Although this study managed to identify the state of cloud computing implementation in Saudi Arabia, its methodology and scope had some shortcomings that limited its generalizability and usability of its findings. For instance, the findings of this study were limited to the SaaS cloud computing service model, which means that other service models of cloud computing including PaaS and IaaS were not studied. Although this may be as a result of primarily SaaS cloud computing implementation in Saudi Arabia, this is not definitive and one cannot determine the extent to which Saudi Arabian companies have applied other forms of services offered by cloud computing service providers. Therefore, any future study should also include the assessment of respondents' understanding of the various cloud computing implementation models to ensure clarity in this matter. In addition, although this study identified the use of some of the services that form the cloud computing package, including email, respondents had difficulties identifying these services as cloud computing, which led to confusion and complications in answering the survey. In this regard, a future study should include clearer definitions and better examples to guide respondents, which may result in more accurate responses and improve the quality of findings. Finally, the sample used for this study, while sufficient in identifying trends, was insufficient to produce representative results that can be accurately generalized to all companies in Saudi Arabia and other geographical regions with shared market environmental factors. Therefore, any future study should have a representative sample that should be calculated from the size of the population of interest.

5.4 Directions for Future Research

In view of the study shortcomings mentioned above, future research should aim at improving knowledge based on the findings of this study, and overcoming the shortcomings of this study. Future studies should cover all aspects of cloud computing, including conventional email to data storage and data management among other advanced forms of cloud computing, which will be instrumental in understanding the people's conception of cloud computing and its importance. Furthermore, future study should expand its scope to account for other implementation and service models of cloud computing, which are going to grow in relevance as the world moves towards the use of remote storage and processing power rather than having local systems. Moreover, a future study that aims to build on the findings of this study should use a bigger sample size, preferably selecting companies based on their industry of operation in an attempt to achieve results that apply for the market in general and can be generalized easily and accurately. In addition, for a future study build on the results of the current study, it should use both qualitative and quantitative data in order to find correlations between various variables in the topic of interest. After other studies have been done for different geographical and cultural environments, one study should consolidate the findings of those studies in order to come up with a unifying theory that explains various trends in the implementation of cloud computing.

5.5 Reflections

Doing this study was quite a challenge, especially due to the scope of the study in terms of the target population and the topic of interest, whereby various factors made the study more challenging more challenging than I anticipated. Nevertheless, the challenges served to prepare me for greater challenge, and enable me to apply the classroom knowledge to a real-life environment that is less than ideal. One of the challenges I faced during the study was that getting businesses to participate in one's study can be really difficult, whereby many of them assume that the researcher has ulterior motives or do not have time to answer questions that have no financial benefits to their operations. In addition, since cloud computing is a relatively recent academic idea, there was limited literature on research done on the topic, which forced me to either use the findings of research that is still in progress, or use whitepapers that offered facts and information without including the methods used in acquiring these facts. In this regard, future research should be focused on growing the knowledge pool for the topic of study to alleviate such shortcomings. Despite these challenges faced in doing this study, doing this research study was quite educational in enabling me to integrate what I have learnt in theoretical classes in the field.

5.6 Learning from this Study

Cloud computing is a relatively modern computing concept, especially in regard to its convergence of existing and emerging computing technologies, and its dependence on internet interconnectivity. In this regard, this study served to put me in the know in regard to recent computing development, which is knowledge that can be applied in my personal and professional life. For instance, I now fully understand the strengths and shortcomings of public cloud computing that may encourage or discourage one from choosing public cloud computing in comparison to other models of cloud computing implementation. In addition, the various cloud computing service models were identified, whereby both secondary and primary research showed that the SaaS model is the most commonly used model based on the needs of users. Moreover, from this study, I understood that availability of resources does not guarantee unlimited availability of a product of service, as is the case of cloud computing in Saudi Arabia that is limited by various factors. Finally, after the interviews with respondents, I found out that, although people do use cloud computing for various business functions and processes, many of them do not understand the concept, especially since many of the services are usually not marketed as cloud computing solutions. Nevertheless, since cloud computing is being adopted by business entities even without full comprehension, this study showed me that cloud computing is feasible and suitable for small and medium-sized businesses in Saudi Arabia despite the obvious shortcomings.

REFERENCES

Aerohive Networks, 2013. *Public or private cloud : The choice is yours.*, s.l.: s.n.

Alali, F. a. &. Y. C.-L., 2012. Cloud computing: Overview and risk analysis. , vol. 26, no. 2(Journal of Information Systems), p. 13–33.

Albeshri, A. & Caelli, W., 2010. Mutual Protection in a Cloud Computing Environment. Issue in 2010 IEEE 12th International Conference on High Performance Computing and Communications (HPCC), p. 641–646.

Ananthi, S. &. K. S., 2012. TPA based cloud storage security techniques. *International Journal of Advanced Research in Computer Engineering & Technology*, Volume vol. 1, no. 8, p. 1–4.

Archives, U. G. -. T. N., 2006. *Small and Medium Enterprise (SME) - Definitions.* [Online] Available at: http://webarchive.nationalarchives.gov.uk/+/http://www.dti.gov.uk/sme4/define.htm [Accessed 7 11 2013].

Armbrust, M. et al., 2010. A view of cloud computing. vol. 53, no. 4,(Communications of the ACM), p. 50–58.

Attas, D. & Batrafi, O., 2011. Efficient integrity checking technique for securing client data in cloud computing. vol. 11, no. 5(International Journal of Electrical & Computer Sciences), p. 43–48.

Awad, R., 2011. Considerations on cloud computing for CPAs. Issue The CPA Journal, no. September, p. 11–13.

Bayrak, E., Conley, J. & & Wilkie, S., 2011. The economics of cloud computing. Volume 11-W18, no. 11.

Beck, T. &. D.-K. A., 2006. Small and medium-size enterprises: Access to finance as a growth constraint. *Journal of Banking & Finance*, vol. 30, no. 11(Elsevier), p. 2931–2943.

Bender, D., 2012. Privacy and security issues in cloud computing. vol. 29, no. 10(The Computer & Internet Lawyer), p. 1–16.

Bowers, L., 2011. *Cloud computing efficiency*, Issue Applied Clinical Trials, pp. 45-51.

Brynjolfsson, E., Hofmann, P. & Jordan, J. a., 2010. *'Cloud computing and electricity: Beyond the utility model', Communications of the ACM, vol. 53, no. 5, pp. 32–34.* [Online] Available at: http://portal.acm.org/citation.cfm?doid=1735223.1735234 [Accessed 18 11 2013].

Buyya, R., J., B. & A., G., 2011. Cloud computing: principles and paradigms. In: New York: John Wiley & Sons.

Chauhan, V., Bansal, K. & & Alappanavar, P., 2012. Exposing cloud computing as a failure. vol. 4, no. 04(International Journal of Engineering Science and Technology), p. 1320–1327.

Chen, W., Yin, K., D, Y. & M, &. H., 2013. *'Data migration from grid to cloud computing', Applied Mathematics & Information Sciences, vol. 406, no. 1, pp. 399–406*. [Online] Available at: http://htwww.naturalspublishing.com/files/published/q6n3lg1769g126.pdf [Accessed 28 11 2013].

Chen, X., Wills, G., Gilbert, L. & Bacigalupo, D., 2010. Technical review of using cloud for research: Guidance notes to cloud infrastructure service providers.

Coutinho, R., 2012. Cloud computing or cloudy computing: are the cost savings worth it?. no. April(Public Management), p. 23.

Cubitt, S., Hassan, R. & & Volkmer, I., 2011. Does cloud computing have a silver lining?. vol. 33, no. 1(Culture & Society), p. 149–158.

Deng, X. et al., 2008. A cross-cultural analysis of the end-user computing satisfaction instrument: A multi-group invariance analysis. vol. 45, no. 4(Information & Management), p. 211–220.

Dixon, H., 2012. Cloud computing. Issue Judges, Journal, vol. 51, no. 2, p. 36038.

Dutta, A., Peng, G. & & Choudhary, A., 2013. Risks in enterprise cloud computing : the perspective of IT experts. vol. 53, no. 4(Journal of Computer Information Systems), p. 39–48.

DynaSis, 2011. Cloud computing: Public, private and hybrid.

Ernst&Young, 2011. Cloud computing issues and impacts. p. 4–56.

Géczy, P., Izumi, N. &. & Hasida, K., 2012. Hybrid cloud considerations: Managerial perspective. vol.29(in 2012 International Conference on Economics, Business and Marketing Management IPEDR), p. 94–97.

Grant AE & Meadows JH, 1. e., 2012. In: *Communication technology update and fundamentals*. s.l.:Taylor & Francis, Boca Raton, FL..

Guion, L., Diehl, D. & McDonald, D., 2011. Triangulation : Establishing the validity of qualitative studies. p. 2–4.

Hastings, R., 2009. Cloud computing. In: *vol. 45, no. 4.* s.l.:Library Technology Reports, pp. 10-12.

Hausman, K. C. S. &. S. T., 2013. Cloud essentials: CompTIA authorized courseware for exam CLO-001. In: Indianapolis: John Wiley & Sons.

Hayes, B., 2008. *'Cloud computing', Communications of the ACM, vol. 51, no. 7, pp. 9–11.* [Online] Available at: http://portal.acm.org/citation.cfm?doid=1364782.1364786 [Accessed 13 11 2013].

Hilley, D., 2009. Cloud Computing: A Taxonomy of Platform and Infrastructure-level Offerings.

Hoefer, C. &. K. G., 2010. Taxonomy of cloud computing services. p. 1345 – 1350.

Hofmann, P. & Woods, D., 2010. *Cloud computing: the limits of public clouds for business applications', IEEE Internet Computing, pp. 90–93.* [Online] Available at: http://ieeexplore.ieee.org/xpls/abs_all.jsp?arnumber=5617066 [Accessed 28 12 2013].

Hugos, M. & Hulitzky, &., 2010. usiness in the cloud: what every business needs to know about cloud computing. In: New York: John Wiley & Sons.

I. C. f. A. I. &., 2013. Under cloud cover: How leaders are accelerating competitive differentiation.

ISACA, 2009. Cloud computing: Business benefits with security, governance and assurance perspectives. Issue Rolling Meadows, IL..

Jamil, D. & Zaki, H., 2011. Cloud computing security. vol. 3, no. 4(International Journal of Engineering Science and Technology), p. 3478–3484.

Jansen, W. &. & Grance, T., 2011. Guidelines on security and privacy in public cloud computing. Issue NIST special publication.

Juster, K., 2008. Cloud computing can close the development gap.

Kalyvas, J., Overly, M. & & Karlyn, M., 2013. Cloud computing : A practical framework for managing cloud computing risk-part 1. vol. 25, no. 3(Intellect Property & Technology Law Journal), p. 7–18.

Karabek, M. K. J. &. P. A., 2011. *Cloud services for SMEs: evolution or revolution?,* 2(Business + Innovation), p. 26–33.

Khan, A., 2012. Access control in cloud computing environment. vol. 7, no. 5(ARPN Journal of Engineering and Applied Sciences), p. 613–615.

Kharat, A., Safvi, A., Thind, S. & & Singh, A., 2012. Cloud computing for radiologists. vol. 22, no. 3(Indian Journal of Radiological Imaging), p. 150–154.

Kshetri, N., 2010. Cloud computing in developing economies: Drivers, effects, and policy measures. p. 1–22.

Kuyoro, S., Ibikunle, F. & Awodele, &., 2011. Cloud computing security issues and challenges. vol. 3, no. 5(International Journal of Computer Networks), p. 247–255.

Leandro, M. et al., 2012. Multi-tenancy authorization system with federated identity for cloud-based environments using shibboleth. Issue in ICN 2012 : The Eleventh International Conference on Networks Multi-Tenancy, p. 88–93.

Lee, Y. & Zomaya, A., 2010. Energy efficient utilization of resources in cloud computing systems. vol. 60, no. 2(The Journal of Supercomputing), p. 268–280.

Leimeister, S., Böhm, M., Riedl, C. & Krcmar, H., 2010. The business perspective of cloud computing: Actors, roles and value networks. Issue in ECIS 2010 Proceedings.

Mahmood, Z. &. H. R., 2011. Cloud computing for enterprise architectures. Issue Springer, London.

Marston, S. L. Z. B. S. Z. J. &. G. A., 2011. *Cloud computing:The business perspective,* Volume vol. 51, no. 1, p. 176–189.

McCourt, M., 2012. Cloud computing. Issue SDM, no. February, pp. 62-70.

Mullender, S., 2012. Predictable cloud computing. vol. 17, no. 2, pp. 25–40.(Bell Labs Technical Journal).

Plummer, D. & Gartner, 2012. The business landscape of cloud computing. pp. 1-40.

Reddy, V. &. R. L., 2011. Security architecture for cloud computing. vol. 3, no. 9(International Journal of Engineering Science and Technology), p. 7149–7156.

Rimal, B., Choi, E. & & Lumb, I., 2009. A taxonomy and survey of cloud computing systems. Issue in 2009 Fifth International Joint Conference on INC, IMS and IDC.

Rosenthal, A. et al., 2010. Cloud computing: A new business paradigm for biomedical information sharing. vol. 43, no. 2(Journal of Biomedical Informatics), p. 342–353.

Ryan, W. & Loeffler, C., 2010. Insights into cloud computing. vol. 22, no. 11(Intellect Property & Technology Law Journa), p. 22–27.

Saboowala, H. A. M. &. M. S., 2013. *Designing networks and services for the cloud: delivering business-grade cloud applications and services,* Issue Cisco Press, Indianapolis.

Saranya, P., Vishnupriya, S. & & Elangovan, E., 2013. Public verifiability and data dynamics in cloud server. vol. 3, no. 3(International Journal of Advanced Technoogy & Engineering Research), p. 78–84.

Schwartz, P., 2013. Information privacy in the cloud. Volume vol. 161, p. 1623–1662.

Science Magazine, 2010. Cloud computing. vol. 19, no. 3(Via Media Ltd., Supply Chain Europe), p. 5.

Skiba, D., 2011. Are you computing in the clouds? Understanding cloud computing. vol. 32, no. 4(Nursing Education Perspectives), p. 266–268.

Smith, R., 2009. Computing in the cloud. Issue Research Technology Management, p. 65–69.

Stair, R. &. R. G., 2010. Fundamentals of information systems, 5th edition. In: Boston: Cengage Learning.

Vacca, J., 2012. Computer and information security handbook, 2nd edition. In: Avenue, NY.: Elsevier Science.

Vimalraj, J. &. & Manoj, M., 2009. Enabling public verifiability and data dynamics for storage security in cloud computing. vol. 04, no. 4(International Journal of Communications and Engineering), p. 20–25.

Wang, Q. et al., 2011. 2011. *Enabling Public Auditability and Data Dynamics for Storage Security in Cloud Computing,* Issue Parallel and Distributed Systems, IEEE Transactions on, p. 847 – 859.

Weber, A., 2011. Cloud computing in education in the Middle East and North Africa (MENA) region: Can barriers be overcome?. Issue in eLearning and Software for Education (eLSE), p. 565–570.

Wessels, T., 2011. What are the benefits of cloud computing? Let's count the ways. Issue New Hampshire Business Review, p. 20.

Yigitbasioglu, O., Mackenzie, K. & & Low, R., 2013. Cloud computing: how does it differ from IT outsourcing and what are the implications for practice and research?. vol. 13, no. April(International Journal of Digital Accounting Research), p. 99–121.

Zamani, A., Akhtar, M. & & Ahmad, S., 2011. Emerging Cloud Computing Paradigm. vol. 8, no. 4(International Journal of Computer Science Issues), p. 304–307.

APPENDICES

Appendix A: Consent Form

Title of Project: Public Cloud Computing in Enterprise Companies in Saudi Arabia: A Feasibility Study

Name of Researcher: [Insert Your Name Here]

1. I confirm that I have read and understand the Plain Language Statement for the above study and have had the opportunity to ask questions.

2. I understand that my participation is voluntary and that I am free to withdraw at any time, without giving any reason.

3. I confirm that my identity will be held in confident, and any information revealing my identity will not be revealed to any unauthorized parties.

4. I understand that my contribution in the focus group discussions will be used in identification of variables for this study, and used to answer the research questions.

5. I agree / do not agree (delete as applicable) to take part in the above study.

Name of Participant   Date   Signature

_____   _____   _____

Researcher   Date   Signature

_____   _____   _____

Appendix B: Plain Language Statement

1. Study title and Researcher Details

Public Cloud Computing in Enterprise Companies in Saudi Arabia: A Feasibility Study

2. Invitation paragraph

You are invited to participate in a face-to-face interview with the researcher for this study. Kindly review the information presented in this statement in order to understand the research, data collection process, importance of the study, and your role in it. Read the information carefully and consult with others if you think it necessary, and ask us in case you need assistance and clarification of the information in this statement. Take your time to make your decision on your willingness or unwillingness to participate in this study.

Thank you for taking your time to read this.

3. What is the purpose of the study?

The purpose of this study will be to determine how feasible the implementation of cloud computing is for enterprise companies in Saudi Arabia.

4. Why have I been chosen?

You have been chosen to participate in this study because your company has implemented public cloud computing over the last 5 years or more, and your input on your experience with the technology will be very much appreciated.

5. Do I have to take part?

Yes, if you agree to participate in the study, you will be expected to contribute but you can withdraw at any time.

6. What will happen to me if I take part?

Your participation in the study will not have any negative effect on you, and, although your participation will be highly appreciated, your identity will not be referenced in presentation of study findings.

7. Will my taking part in this study be kept confidential?

The information collected from you and your company will only be accessible to the interviewer, and it will not contain any identifying information for you or your company.

8. What will happen to the results of the research study?

The results of this study will be used to compile factors related to the research topic, which will then be used to answer the research questions and make recommendations.

9. Who has reviewed the study?

[Insert Manager's Name Here]

10. Contact for Further Information

[Insert Your Name and Contact]

11. Contact for Concerns regarding Conduct of the Research

[Insert Name of Institutional Research-Officer-in-Charge]

Appendix C: Semi-Structured Questionnaire

1. Kindly tell me something about your company, including ownership, shareholding and the decision making process.

2. What cloud computing services does your company implement?

3. What factors necessitated the implementation of cloud computing in your company?

4. Did you consider multiple alternatives to cloud computing?

5. If the answer to '2' above is yes, why did you choose public cloud computing?

6. What properties did you seek in an ideal service provider?

7. What challenges did you experience during and after implementation?

8. How did you overcome the challenges mentioned in '7' above?

9. Did cloud computing affect your production and service delivery? Kindly explain.

10. What was the effect of cloud computing on employee output?

11. What was the effect of cloud computing on the costs of running business for your company?

12. What was the effect of cloud computing on your company's revenue?

13. Do your company's fortunes look better than they would have been without cloud computing?

Appendix D: Interview Schedule

Day	Company									
	1	2	3	4	5	6	7	8	9	10
Sun 19th Jan	███	███								
Mon 20th Jan			███	███						
Tue 21th Jan					███	███				
Wed 22th Jan							███	███		
Thu 23th Jan									███	███

www.ingramcontent.com/pod-product-compliance
Lightning Source LLC
LaVergne TN
LVHW042257060326
832902LV00009B/1099